T0132075

# How Can God Be a Rock?

A Children's Guide to Idioms in the Bible

Dr. Janielle Nordell, MD

Edited by Isaiah Nordell

# FOREWORD

Thank you so much for reading our book! As a pediatrician, I have had the pleasure of working closely with children and their families and learning how children develop. Every child grows differently, and I continue to be amazed at how wonderful and unique God has made each and every one. As a mom, I have also watched my own children learn about life and God in contrasting ways, just as they are gifted to naturally excel at different things. While one child may grasp imaginative play and figures of speech naturally, my other child is a very intelligent but literal thinker. Thinking more literally is especially common for younger children and those on the autism spectrum.

Can you imagine how confusing it can be for a literal thinker - or even a young thinker in general - to interpret figures of speech? Why do we even use the expression, "It's raining cats and dogs?" It rains water, not animals! These figures of speech are not only used in our everyday speech, but also throughout the Bible. Idioms, such as "He is my rock," are more difficult to understand. Yet we use them constantly.

One day on our way to church, we were all listening to Bible songs. One song stood out to me: "The Word of the Lord will stand forever" from 1 Peter 1:24. Knowing how my children think differently, I asked my son, Isaiah, what he thought that meant. He could not explain it to me. He told me it did not make sense, because a book cannot stand on feet. We talked through it, laughed about the ridiculousness of a standing Bible, and continued on. But then I thought how wonderful it would be for children like Isaiah to have a reference guide that explained such figures of speech in a way they could understand. I searched everywhere and couldn't find such a guide. So I decided to write one and have Isaiah help explain them with me. These are just a few of the many verses we've found. We hope you enjoy it, and that it "sheds light" on what God is telling us in His Bible!

DARKNESS

LIGHT (of Life)

**John 8:12 - Then Jesus again spoke to them, saying, "I am the Light of the world; he who follows Me will not walk in the darkness, but will have the Light of Life."**

Jesus is the Light of the world. What does this mean? He isn't the sun or a light bulb from a lamp. That is silly, right? When it is all dark at night with no light, you feel all alone and scared. But when the light turns on, you can see! You know where you are and what is around you. You don't have to be scared anymore. You can see where you need to go. Jesus helps you see the right way to go. He helps you feel safe and happy, just like light does.

**John 6:35 - Jesus said to them, "I am the bread of life; he who comes to Me will not hunger, and he who believes in Me will never thirst."**

What in the world?! Bread of Life? Jesus isn't a piece of bread. What does this mean? We need to eat food every day to stay alive. God makes sure you have real bread and other things you need - food, clothes, a home, and so much more. He not only takes care of us on earth, but He also makes sure we can always be with Him. If you trust in Jesus, you will go to heaven. Both bread and Jesus help you stay alive - bread here on earth for your body, and Jesus to live with Him forever.

ROCK =
GOD

**Psalm 62:2 - He only is my Rock and my salvation, my Stronghold; I shall not be greatly shaken.**

God isn't actually a rock. That is crazy! Rocks don't love us like God does. BUT rocks are stable and strong. When you are in a house built on a rock, you are SAFE. If a storm comes, and you aren't on a rock, you are in danger. God keeps us safe, and He protects us, just like a big rock can.

PATIENCE
HUMILITY
KINDNESS
COMPASSION
LOVE
GENTLENESS

**Colossians 3:12, 14 - Clothe yourselves with compassion, kindness, humility, gentleness and patience... and over all these virtues put on love, which binds them all together in perfect unity.**

Do you think God means these big words are clothes we wear, like dresses, belts, shirts, or pants? No!! We cannot wear words on our bodies. Sometimes we say "clothe" when we talk about things that aren't clothes. Why? Clothes are the first thing people see when they look at you. People also see how we act and treat other people. These big words are things God wants us to be doing all of the time:

COMPASSION - wanting to help someone who needs help
KINDNESS - being nice
HUMILITY - not bragging or thinking you are better than other people
GENTLENESS - being kind and careful
PATIENCE - waiting calmly and without complaining
LOVE - always making someone or something in your life to be very important

When a person looks at you, they should first see that your actions show these things.

**Colossians 3:13 - Bear with each other and forgive one another if any of you has a grievance against someone. Forgive as the Lord forgave you.**

What do you think "bear with each other" means? Does it mean play teddy bears with each other? No, that is silly! This time, "bear" isn't talking about the animal. It means to help each other and do things to make their life better. Do you feel better when your mom helps you carry a heavy bag from the car? What if you help a friend find their lost toy? Of course! You should "bear" it and help someone when they have a lot to do or to carry. You could also help someone when they feel sad or lonely. If they hurt your feelings, you should forgive them and keep loving and caring for them.

**Psalm 128:1 - Blessed are all who fear the Lord, who walk in His ways!**

Should we be afraid of God? No way!! Sometimes the word "fear" means to respect, or to be amazed by something. When we respect God, we want to do what He tells us to do.

Do you think God is telling us to find the same trails on a dirt road that Jesus walked on so long ago? I don't think so. We would have to travel to a place very far away to actually walk where He did. To "walk in His ways" means to follow His example. Have you ever heard someone say, "follow in his footsteps"? It is the same - to copy that person. If we copy Jesus, it means we are acting and talking like Him. By doing this, we show God respect, and this leads to rewards. Who wants a reward from God? I want one!

**Isaiah 43:2 - When you walk through fire you will not be burned, and the flame will not set you ablaze.**

Have you ever walked in a real fire? I hope not. Have you ever gotten burned? It really hurts, doesn't it? Fire can burn and hurt you, so why does God say you can walk through fire and not get hurt? He's not telling us to go in a real fire. He is saying that He protects you when life is hard. He protects us because He loves us and He is always with us, even though you can't see Him. God is like a firefighter who keeps you safe in a real fire. You are always safe with God.

BIBLE

**Isaiah 40:8 - The grass withers, the flower fades, but the Word of our God stands forever.**

What is the "Word of God"? This is another way to talk about the Bible. God is the author of the Bible. The words on its pages are from Him! But what does it mean that the Word of God STANDS forever? Do Bibles have real feet to stand on? No way! That is crazy talk. Sometimes the word "stand" means to stay true and strong, and to never go away. Grass does not live forever. Flowers die, too. But the Bible will never go away and will always be true.

**Matthew 7:7-8 - Ask and it will be given to you; seek and you will find; knock and the door will be opened to you. For everyone who asks receives; the one who seeks finds; and to the one who knocks, the door will be opened.**

Is this verse telling us to play hide and seek with God? I wish this were true, because that would be so much fun!! Do you think it is talking about a magic door we actually need to knock on? No. But what does this all mean? A lot of times, we forget to ask God for His help when we have a hard time, or we forget to ask for help to do something that is very hard to do. This is what it really means when Jesus says to "seek" Him. When you go to a friend's house to play, how do you get inside to play? You have to knock on the door and ask to go in. Then you get to do what you asked for - to play with your friend.

God is never hiding from you. He is waiting for you to ask Him for help. When you pray, it is like knocking on God's door. Praying is talking with God. Talking with God will help you do what you thought was too hard. Just ask Him for help.

DANGER

**John 15:3 - Greater love has no one than this: to lay down one's life for his friends.**

Does this mean that laying down in bed makes you a good friend? No! Taking a nap has nothing to do with how to be a good friend. How can you be a good friend? You give up something you like so they can do what they want to do. If they want to play a game you don't want to, you choose to play their game because you love them. You give up what you like because you care for and love your friend. You can also show love for your family. If your mom asks you to do your chores, you show that you love your mom by doing what she asks you to do. When we give up what we want in order to show love to other people, we are copying some of what Jesus did for us.

What does it mean to "lay down one's life"? This means you die to save your friend, just like Jesus did for you and me. The best kind of love is being willing to die for your friend so they can live. This is what Jesus did for you and me! He loves you, and He is your greatest friend.

WestBow Press books may be ordered through booksellers or by contacting:

WestBow Press
A Division of Thomas Nelson & Zondervan
1663 Liberty Drive
Bloomington, IN 47403
www.westbowpress.com
1 (866) 928-1240



ISBN: 978-1-9736-5997-6 (sc)
ISBN: 978-1-9736-5998-3 (e)

Library of Congress Control Number: 2019904232

Print information available on the last page.

WestBow Press rev. date: 04/25/2019

Printed in the United States
By Bookmasters